The 30 Day Whole Food Challenge

Whole Foods Diet - Whole Foods Cookbook & Whole Food Recipes

The 30 Day Whole Food Challenge

© Copyright 2016 - All rights reserved.

The contents of this book may not be reproduced, duplicated or transmitted without direct written permission from the author.

Under no circumstances will any legal responsibility or blame be held against the publisher for any reparation, damages, or monetary loss due to the information herein, either directly or indirectly.

Legal Notice:

This book is copyright protected. This is only for personal use. You cannot amend, distribute, sell, use, quote or paraphrase any part or the content within this book without the consent of the author.

Disclaimer Notice:

Please note the information contained within this document is for educational and entertainment purposes only. Every attempt has been made to provide accurate, up to date and reliable complete information. No warranties of any kind are expressed or implied. Readers acknowledge that the author is not engaging in the rendering of legal, financial, medical or professional advice. The content of this book has been derived from various sources. Please consult a licensed professional before attempting any techniques outlined in this book.

The 30 Day Whole Food Challenge

By reading this document, the reader agrees that under no circumstances are is the author responsible for any losses, direct or indirect, which are incurred as a result of the use of information contained within this document, including, but not limited to, —errors, omissions, or inaccuracies.

The 30 Day Whole Food Challenge

Table of Contents

INTRODUCTION	XI
CHAPTER 1: THE WHOLE FOODS DIET EXPLAINED	1
Whole foods vs. processed foods	1
What happens to processed foods?	2
What the whole foods diet incorporates	3
Cooking whole foods	4
CHAPTER 2: WHAT ARE THE BENEFITS OF THE WHOLE FOODS DIET?	5
Health benefits of the whole foods diet	5
CHAPTER 3: WHAT CAN IT DO AND CANNOT DO?	10
What it can do for you	10
What it cannot do for you	11
CHAPTER 4: THE HISTORY OF IT – HOW IT CAME TO BE	14
CHAPTER 5: HOW YOU CAN GET STARTED?	19
Research	19

The 30 Day Whole Food Challenge

Shopping list ... 19

Pantry restocking ... 20

Recipe books ... 20

Health check ... 20

Goals ... 21

Reward yourself ... 21

Inform people ... 21

Partner up ... 22

Speak out ... 22

CHAPTER 6: WHOLE FOODS DIPS AND SPREADS ... 24

Tahini ... 24

Carrot n Cashew Spread ... 25

Hummus ... 26

Walnut Feta Cheese Dip ... 27

Guacamole ... 28

Lemon Ricotta Kale Dip ... 29

Chipotle Chili Bean Dip ... 30

Mayonnaise ... 31

CHAPTER 7: WHOLE FOOD BREAKFAST RECIPES — 32

Savory Sausage and Cheddar Breakfast Casserole — 32

Cauliflower Pancakes — 33

Blueberry & Toasted Almond Muesli — 35

Quinoa Breakfast Bowl — 36

Green Egg Skillet Bake — 38

Scrambled Tofu — 40

Grilled Vegetable Panzanella — 41

CHAPTER 8: SMOOTHIES RECIPES — 43

Strawberry Almond Butter Smoothie — 43

Rainbow Chard Ginger Fruit Smoothie — 44

Pineapple Breeze Smoothie — 45

Kale n Berry Smoothie — 46

Mixed Fruit Smoothie — 47

Fig Smoothie — 48

CHAPTER 9: WHOLE FOOD SOUP RECIPES — 49

Lentil soup — 49

Mushroom soup — 50

The 30 Day Whole Food Challenge

Golden Squash Curry Soup	51
Seafood Gazpacho	53
Mexican Soup	54
Tofu Noodle Soup	56
Kale Soup	57
Thai Chicken Soup	58
French Onion Soup	60
Beef Stew	61
CHAPTER 10: WHOLE FOODS SALAD RECIPES	63
Rainbow Soba Salad	63
Arugula, Grape, and Sunflower Seed Salad	64
Mango Quinoa Salad	65
Black Beans and Corn Salad	66
Caper and Lemon Salad	67
Summer Salad	68
Caribbean Chicken Salad	69
Detox Salad	71

CHAPTER 11: WHOLE FOODS SNACK RECIPES — 72

Roast potatoes in mint gravy — 72

Steamed samosas — 73

Spicy chicken patties — 74

Chickpea stuffed flat bread — 76

Spicy Pumpkin Seeds / Nuts — 78

Apple Sandwiches with Granola and Peanut Butter — 79

Kale Chips/Zucchini — 80

Cucumber Boats — 81

Crispy Edamame Popcorn — 82

Almond Butter Energy Balls — 83

Blueberry Basil Muffins — 84

Pita Pizza — 86

CHAPTER 12: WHOLE FOODS MAIN COURSE - MEAT RECIPES — 88

Curried Chicken Over Spinach — 88

Chicken Kebabs with Tomato-Parsley Salad — 90

Grilled Salmon and Lemon with Herbs — 91

Curried Shrimp — 92

Coconut Red Pork Curry — 93

Grilled Teriyaki Pork Lettuce Wraps — 95

Healthy Turkey Meatloaf — 96

Rosemary Lamb Chops — 98

Beef Taco Pizza — 99

CHAPTER 13: WHOLE FOODS VEGETARIAN RECIPES — 100

Mushroom Stroganoff — 100

Spicy Black Bean Burrito — 102

Asian Sautéed Cauliflower — 103

Herbed Potatoes — 104

Spinach Hummus Pinwheel Wraps — 105

CHAPTER 14: WHOLE FOOD SANDWICH RECIPES — 106

Cuban Sandwich — 106

Turkey Sandwich — 107

Open Face Apple Tahini Sandwich — 108

Homemade Burgers — 109

CHAPTER 15: WHOLE FOODS INFUSED WATER — 110

Lemon ginger water — 110

Strawberry basil water — 111

Spicy water — 112

Grapefruit infusion — 113

Melon and ginger infusion — 114

Banana and Honey infusion — 115

Green water — 116

Blueberry and melon infusion — 117

Cucumber lemon ginger infusion — 118

Rose petal infusion — 119

Kiwi and rosemary infusion — 120

CONCLUSION — 121

The 30 Day Whole Food Challenge

Introduction

Diet plays a key role in promoting a person's good health and it is essential to follow a healthy diet to stave off illnesses and prolong one's life.

However, people's health has taken a severe hit, owing to hectic lifestyles and over dependence on processed foods. Right from obesity to cardiovascular illnesses, everybody has one health complaint or the other and continuing on the same path will only lead to self-destruction. It is therefore important for people to mend their ways and take up a diet that will allow them to improve their health and attain vital vigor.

One way of doing so is by taking up the whole foods diet. It is a type of diet that promotes the consumption of whole foods while leaving out processed foods. In this book, we will look at the diet in detail and understand its various aspects. There are also many recipes provided in this book, which will make it easier for you to start off on the diet.

The diet is easy to follow and anybody can take it up. All that you are required to do is try it for a month and look at the difference that it makes. Once you are convinced you will not return back to your regular diet.

Let's begin.

Chapter 1: The Whole Foods Diet Explained

For all those people keen on fixing up their health and developing a strong and lean body, the whole foods diet makes for an excellent choice.

As we know, stress, pollution and junk foods bring harm to our bodies and can induce various illnesses. It is therefore important to take matters in our own hands and adopt a lifestyle, diet and exercise routine that will allow us to lead a better life.

Whole foods vs. processed foods

Whole foods basically include all those foods that have not been touched by factories. They are available in their raw state and very little to nothing has been done to them. The whole foods diet is now widely accepted as one that promotes overall health and vigor. It is generally followed by athletes in order to maintain a slim and healthy body.

On the other hand, processed foods are all those that are altered by food companies and contain tons of harmful chemicals. These chemicals are capable of damaging our bodies and will take a very long time for us to heal. It is therefore best to avoid consumption of these foods and switch over to whole foods. Processed foods are generally put through a long process and end up losing most of their nutritional values. The processes often tend to strip off the nutrients and replace them with harmful chemicals.

Anything that comes in a box or a bag or is canned or comes out of a jar is processed is not considered to be whole foods. These can be considered as whole foods that are broken down in order to process them before being sold in stores.

What happens to processed foods?

Foods are generally processed to achieve any one or all of the following effects:

- Color- artificial color is added to foods to enhance their appearance. These colors are mostly carcinogenic in nature.
- Stabilize – stabilizers are added to thicken the sauces and pastes. These are laden with harmful chemicals.
- Emulsify – These are added in to combine the different components of the product.
- Bleach – bleach is added in to remove any odors and also to prevent the growth of bacteria.
- Texturize – certain ingredients are added in to texturize the food substance.
- Soften – some substances are added in to soften the ingredients in the foods.
- Preserve – preservatives are added to foods to prolong their shelf life. They contain extremely harmful chemicals.
- Sweeten – chemicals are added in place of sugar to make the foods extremely sweet. Some are also

laden with excess amounts of sugar such as sodas and candies.
- Flavor – artificial flavorings are not derived from natural food substances and come from chemicals that mimic the taste of these substances thereby making them extremely unhealthy.
- Processed foods also contain lots of sodium owing to the addition of salt as a preservative.
- They contain monounsaturated and polyunsaturated fats that are capable of clogging up the arteries and giving your heart a tough time.
- Most processed foods contain traces of allergens that are capable of triggering off an allergic reaction.
- These foods are basically high in calorific content and low in fiber and nutritional content which makes them extremely unhealthy choices for people.

Regular consumption of foods having gone through these processes can cause bodies to develop cancer, cardiovascular diseases and obesity. In fact, the WHO attributes a spike in obesity to the consumption of junk foods.

What the whole foods diet incorporates

You can incorporate all those things that are not processed including fresh fruits and vegetables, beans, seeds, lentils, oats, wheat, barley, eggs, poultry, red meat and seafood. You must avoid processed foods such as chips, cakes, sodas, canned juices, canned vegetables, dehydrated vegetables, frozen meats, sauces and condiments. These are all processed to change their taste and appearance and can be extremely unhealthy.

Cooking whole foods

It is a fact that we ourselves are guilty of processing foods to a certain extent, while cooking them. But, we do not necessarily process it to add in chemicals and other harmful substances. We only tenderize the food to make it a bit more palatable. However, there are many drawbacks to over cooking whole foods, as their nutritional value can deplete. It is therefore best to cook them for the right amounts of time, so that their nutritional values can be preserved. You can make use of a slow cooker to cook the whole foods, as it is capable of cooking the food thoroughly while still preserving the basic nutrients.

Chapter 2: What Are The Benefits Of The Whole Foods Diet?

The whole foods diet introduces to the body a whole host of health benefits some of which are discussed below.

Health benefits of the whole foods diet

Heart health

When it comes to maintaining a fit body, heart health should be given primary importance, as it is the most important organ of the body. You have to pay attention to what you eat, as everything has a direct bearing on your heart's health. Certain whole foods are rich in omega 3 fatty acids and other amino acids that keep your heart health in check. You can also successfully reduce the presence of bad cholesterol in your body and increase your chances of beating the onset of cardio vascular ailments. But you have to supplement the diet with regular exercise to ensure that you give your body a chance to attain optimum heart health. Seafood, flax seeds and oats are all great for your heart's health.

Liver/ gut health

It is extremely important for you to take good care of your liver as it contains the first line of defense against diseases. Known as Kupffer cells, the liver is lined with these tiny cells, which unleash anti-bodies after sensing a threat. However, if you overload your liver with the work of sorting out complex chemicals, then it will deteriorate in function and not be able to release the anti-bodies fast enough. It is therefore important for you to consume whole foods as they make it easier for your liver to digest the nutrients without having to put in too much effort. The gut supplements the liver in function and by consuming whole foods; you successfully introduce all those nutrients that are capable of staving off the leaky gut syndrome. Try consuming beans and wheat as both are known to promote liver health.

Kidney health

Kidneys are chiefly responsible for purifying the blood in your body, which makes for an extremely important bodily function. You have to consume foods that will work on both enhancing your kidney's function and also lessen its work. Many nutrients present in whole foods will mix with your blood and purify it by fighting away pathogens and other toxins. This will take away some of the load from your kidneys and help you optimize their function. Consuming kidney beans and tomatoes will improve your kidney health considerably.

Digestion

Whole foods are extremely rich in fiber, which is required by the body to digest food. Fiber is not digested by the body and passes out whole. But the body is fooled into thinking that it is possible to digest it and makes an extra effort to break it down. This helps in increasing metabolism and also burns calories. By consuming whole foods, you will reduce the occurrence of an upset stomach and have the chance to improve your appetite. Consuming fresh fruits and vegetables such as apples, bananas, beans and carrots will aid in digestion.

Hormones

Erratic lifestyle choices are now causing more and more people to develop hormonal imbalances. The only way to fix this problem is by taking up the whole foods diet. You have to consume foods that are rich in hormone balancing nutrients such as folic acid. You should try to incorporate leafy green vegetables and orange juice in your diet, as both of these are rich in hormone enhancing nutrients. Make it a point to gulp down a glass of orange juice every morning as that will help your body in many different ways.

Muscles

This diet is also ideal for thin people as whole foods are rich in proteins. Proteins aid in the development of strong muscles, which is requisite to bulk up. Just by consuming whole foods such as chicken, eggs and turkey a person can successfully introduce a lot of proteins into their systems.

Immunity

As you know, prevention is better than cure and it is important for you to shield your body against illnesses. Whole foods contain phytochemicals that are plant based and designed to strengthen your body from the inside out. These phytochemicals will prepare your body to combat illnesses and promote good health. You have to ensure that you consume foods rich in anti-oxidants such as apples, oranges, green leafy vegetables and also green tea.

Cancers

The elimination of chemicals from your diet is a big step towards cutting down on the risk of developing certain types of cancers. The whole food diet strictly prohibits the consumption of junk and processed foods that can contain carcinogens. Foods rich in anti-oxidants will reduce oxidative damage to a large extent and promote optimal health.

Longevity

It is possible for you to live a longer life when you take up the whole foods diet. Whole food Diets such as the Mediterranean diet are known to help people live longer. The foods are free from chemicals and are not over processed, which helps in maintaining the vital nutrients required by the body. Consuming these will help in the development of healthy cells capable of keeping your body fit for longer. But you must also supplement the diet with a proper exercise routine, as it will go a long way in helping you further enhance your longevity.

Mental health

Stress is now a major cause for people to develop mental illnesses such as anxiety and depression. Both of these can have a long-term impact on the person's brain and so it is extremely important to put an end to it as soon as possible and can be achieved through the consumption of whole foods. They contain amino acids such as tryptophan and vitamin B, both of which are chiefly responsible for the release of the happiness hormone known as serotonin. You can prevent the onset of illnesses such as Alzheimer's and dementia just by consuming whole foods while taking a break from processed foods.

Skin/hair/nails

The whole food diet is extremely efficient in enhancing skin, hair and nail health. You can consume foods that are rich in folic acid, proteins and vitamins E and C to enhance your outward appearance.

These are just some of the health benefits that the whole foods diet can give to your body and is not limited to just these. You will have the chance to come face to face with the others as and when you take up the diet.

Chapter 3: What Can It Do And Cannot Do?

The whole foods diet is quite healthy and can do a lot of things for your body. However, it is not a cure-all and comes with its own set of limitations. Here are the things that the diet can do for you and also what it cannot.

What it can do for you

The whole foods diet introduces a whole host of nutrients to your body including vitamins, minerals, amino acids, fiber etc. It also introduces those vital substances to the body that are not produced within it. So just by taking up the whole food diet you end up exposing your body to all the requisite nutrients it will need to stay strong and healthy for a lifetime.

Our bodies require 22 vital amino acids and 9 of which are not produced inside the body. One such acid is known as valine, which is required to process muscle metabolism and also repair the tissues inside the body. This acid is supplied by whole foods such as beef, beans and lentils. You have to incorporate them into your diet as much as possible and try to avoid buying products that process these foods.

Most researchers and doctors compare the whole foods diet to the ones that our ancestors followed. They were able to lead healthier lives owing to consuming whole foods that were not processed and were free from chemicals. You too can avail the same benefits by cutting out on the processed and junk foods and give your body the chance to avail a natural synergy by consuming whole foods.

Since most whole foods are derived from plants, they are rich in phytochemicals required by our body to remain healthy. They are designed to combat illnesses and also prevent the body from aging fast.

Whole foods are laden with anti-oxidants that are a vital component to maintaining good health. They aid in cutting down on the free radicles that float inside your body and promote the growth of healthy cells. Just by switching to whole foods, you can successfully increase chances of beating many types of cancers

These foods not only work on the inside of your body but also on the outside. In the previous chapter, we already looked at the various health benefits that the diet can provide your body and why it is a great idea for you to switch to it from your regular diet. In this next segment, we will look at some limitations of the whole foods diet.

What it cannot do for you

Overnight results

Do not expect to lose oodles of weight on an overnight basis. It is not possible to do so and will take you some time to notice a change in your body. You have to set yourself reasonable goals and ensure that you measure your progress from time to time. You should write down your health goals and strike them off one by one over the course of 6 months to a year.

Cure illnesses

The whole foods diet can stave off the onset of an illness but might not be able to reverse one that you are already suffering from. It might mitigate the illness to a large extent but not cure it. You have to have reasonable expectations from the diet and not pin too much hope on its effects on the illness. It can be considered as a great supplement to the medication you are consuming to control the illness.

Make up the lack of exercise

cannot forgo exercising just because you are on the whole foods diet. The diet will not cut down on your fat, which can only be achieved through proper exercise. You can choose a routine that will suit your body type and help you to both cut down on the fat and also dissolve it to be eliminated from your body. You can take up 1 hour of light exercise or 30 minutes of rigorous exercise on a daily basis to combat the amount of fat deposited in your body.

Cut down calories

Certain plant based foods are capable of containing excess amounts of calories and it is important for you to note which ones are good for you and which ones are best avoided. Starchy vegetables and fruits such as potatoes contain lots of carbs that can cause your body to remain with lots of energy that is not easily burned away. It is important for you to make a list of these and avoid consuming them as much as possible.

Curb Gluten consumption

Many whole foods such as oats, barley and wheat contain gluten, which can be bad for certain people, especially the ones suffering from celiac disease. You must run a test to check if you have it and avoid consuming the foods that are laden with gluten.

Supplements

Although you will get most of the essential nutrients from whole foods, you might have to consume some supplements to avail the rest of them. You can speak with your doctor to know which ones you need to consume in order to supplement your body's requirements.

Chapter 4: The History Of It – How It Came To Be

Our ancestors, the Neanderthals and Paleoliths consumed a diet that was extremely nutritious. This contributed towards them developing a strong and healthy body. But the same, sadly, cannot be said about modern man, as he is exposed to all types of chemical laden food substances.

Processed foods came into being around 250 years ago, when the food industry decided to change the face of American diets. Processed foods were seen as cheaper and better alternatives to whole foods, as all that people had to do was open up a packet and start eating out from it. Although it was initially just an urban phenomenon, the rural population also took to it and exploited it just as much, if not more.

Natural foods slowly began to get replaced by processed foods as industries manufacturing these foods began to mushroom all over America. By the year 1860, processed foods became a staple in most American households who preferred to eat out of cans and jars. Companies that manufactured these products did not care for people's health and decided to sell their products on a large scale. They even advertised these processed foods as being nutritious and healthful, which further prompted the masses to switch over.

As their profits began to grow, people's health began to deteriorate. It was obvious that being exposed to foods lacking nutritional value and containing high levels of toxins was weakening people's immune systems and making them susceptible to illnesses. By the year 1900, most of the population was struggling with digestive problems and health issues owing to the consumption of processed foods. Several diseases were rampant as people cut out whole foods and consumed foods out of cans and jars.

Digestive disorders had suddenly become the most common cause for deaths in the US and people were still not aware that it was the canning and dehydrating of their foods that was causing it. Many fraudulent drug companies promised to cure the conditions, which further added to the problem at hand. The government at the time tried to control the problem by passing laws against such companies. But people were too blinded by advertising to separate the right from the wrongs.

The government failed to realize that they had to pass laws against the companies that produced the processed foods and not the medics who tried to sell placebos to the masses.

After being slaves to the processed foods for almost 130 years, many Americans decided to abandon it and pick up healthier habits. Although it took them a very long time to realize it, they did manage to switch over to a healthier habit.

They realized that the only way to get healthy and stave off illnesses was to consume a diet that was plant based. They started mimicking the diets that our ancestors followed and came up with the concept of vegan and Paleo diets. The vegan diet is one that promotes the consumption of organic foods that are grown in organic farms. They also emphasize on slow cooking at low temperatures as it allows you to trap the nutritional content within the foods.

The Paleo diet mimics the food pattern that Paleoliths followed. It bans the consumption of all those foods that modern man is exposed to including junk and processed foods. It also bans the consumption of seeds and lentils, as Paleo man did not have access to it. They are of the belief that our digestive system is incapable of digesting such foods and so, it is best to shift to a diet that does not encourage their consumption.

But not all have managed to reform and the trend sadly continues even today. There are many who don't realize the importance of switching over to whole foods.

They continue to depend on foods that come out of cans and jars and it is obvious that continuing on the same path will only lead to a country that has a majority of obese people, all suffering from various illnesses.

Many people have questioned the efficacy of the whole food diets owing to a spurt in fad diets and how they often don't work well. However, the whole foods diet should be considered a lifestyle choice and not just a temporary food habit.

You have to think of it as more of a regular diet you will have to stick with for the rest of your life. It is the only way in which you can save your body and put an end to the onset of illnesses.

In the next chapter, we will look at the things that you can do to start off with and stick with the diet.

Here are the nutritional values that you can avail if you shift from the processed food diet to the whole foods diet.

- Your body will be able to process and synthesize proteins in a better manner. It will be sent to all the right body parts and you won't have to worry about it not being synthesized efficiently.
- Your body can avail a lot of great enzymes that are important for optimal functioning.
- You will expose your body to many vitamins that are capable of improving your overall health. These vitamins in fact are necessary to increase your body's capacity to meet every day nutritional requirements.
- The minerals that the whole food diet adds to your body will make you stronger from the inside. These include zinc, iron and phosphorous. These are not produced within the body and so it is important to avail them through food sources.

- Essential Fatty Acids are also a requisite and can be availed through whole foods. Your heart will remain healthier for longer if you consume these acids on a regular basis.
- You can avail beneficial microflora that is required by your digestive system. Once your digestive health improves, your overall health will quickly follow suit.

Chapter 5: How you can get Started?

It is often difficult to introduce a radical change in the diet and requires one to go about it in a planned manner. Remember that you should consider it a lifestyle choice and not just a temporary food habit.

If you are keen on taking up the whole foods diet on a permanent basis then here are some pointers that will help you with your journey.

Research

It is extremely important for you to conduct a thorough research on the topic in order to prepare your mind and body for the diet. This book will provide you with enough information, no doubt, but you must not limit yourself to this alone. You can turn to other sources as well to garner as much information on the topic as possible in order to heighten your awareness and adopt a sustainable diet that can help you regain your health and vigor. But make sure you look at reliable sources and keep away from spurious ones.

Shopping list

The next thing to do is to make a shopping list and incorporate all the whole foods that are allowed as per the diet. We looked at the ones that are allowed and also the banned items and you can constitute your list based on the same. You can create a list and save it so that it can be easily pulled up every time you plan to go shopping. You can also shop online if you think it might tempt you to hit the processed food aisles at the supermarket. Visiting an organic market is a good idea as they generally stock up on whole foods.

Pantry restocking

Next, throw out everything that is not allowed in the diet and replace them with the whole foods that you buy. If some of the food is still good then you can give it away to friends and family. There is no room for cheat meals as per the whole foods diet so it is best for you to do away with all the processed and junk foods present in your house. You should also clear out your fridge before restocking it with whole foods. In case you are in the habit of shopping for an entire month, you can buy large boxes to store all the whole foods.

Recipe books

You will have to buy some good recipe books to keep you inspired. This book will give you many recipes no doubt but you must not limit yourself to just these. You can download other books from the Internet or look for good ones at a bookstore. It pays to have a few recipes handy so that you don't feel lazy or monotonous.

Health check

Before you start with the diet, it is best to get your health checked. Even though the whole foods diet is extremely healthy it is important for you to check your vital statistics. The doctor might run a few tests to check your overall health and see if you require any supplements. If you consume any medication then he might have to change it up to suit your new requirements. Once you take up the diet, you must visit the doctor regularly to see how it is working out for you.

Goals

Setting health goals will help you stay on course. You can make a list of goals to attain and go after them one by one. Most people choose to set both long term and short-term goals so they can go about it in a systematic manner. You too can do the same and set yourself both 6 months and weekly health goals. But make sure that they are reasonable, as setting unreasonable goals can throw you off track.

Reward yourself

It is a good idea for you to reward yourself from time to time. This is especially important if you wish to remain motivated and stick with the diet. The reward can be a material possession like a new camera or a healthy meal at your favorite restaurant. But don't reward yourself too often as it will lose its value and you will get used to it.

Inform people

It is best to inform people around you that you are taking up the whole foods diet so that you can avoid answering awkward questions. You might have to carry your own meals to office and also to restaurants and is best to tell everyone in advance. You can also inform the host of parties that you attend about your diet and get them to prepare a separate menu for you.

Partner up

You can find yourself a partner to take up the diet with you. Having a partner helps in remaining motivated and the two of you can encourage each other to stick with it for life. The two of you can also join a whole foods group where people discuss about the diet and share tips. If no such group exists then you can start one by yourself. Use social media to tell people about it and invite them over to discuss the topic with you.

Speak out

Talking about your health goals and professing about the goodness of the diet can all help you stick with it for a longer time. You should make an effort to maintain a blog chronicling your journey and refer to it from time to time to look at your progress. You can come in contact with others who are following the same diet and exchange tips and recipes.

These are just some things that you can do to start and maintain the diet and apart from these, you can also take up other activities that you think will work for you.

In the next few chapters, I have collated a 30 days meal plan for you, which includes recipes for different meal times and snacks that you can consume to make this diet a success.

Chapter 6: Whole Foods Dips and Spreads

Tahini

Ingredients:
- 2 cups sesame seeds, hulled
- 1/4 cup olive oil or more if required

Method:
1. Heat a heavy skillet over medium heat. Add sesame seeds. Sauté until they are golden brown. Do not burn them. Remove from heat and keep aside to cool.
2. Place the sesame seeds in a food processor. Add about 1/4 cup olive oil. Blend to make a paste. Add more live oil if you find the paste is too thick and blend again.
3. Store in an airtight jar in the refrigerator. It can store for many months in the refrigerator.

Carrot n Cashew Spread

Ingredients:
- 2 medium carrots, chopped
- 1/2 cup cashew pieces
- 1/4 cup dried apricots, chopped

Method:
1. Place a small pot of water over medium heat. Add carrots and bring to a boil.
2. Lower heat and simmer until carrots are tender.
3. Add 6 tablespoons cashew and apricots and cook for another 6-7 minutes.
4. Retain about 1/2 a cup of the cooked liquid and drain the remaining.
5. Blend together carrots, cashews, apricots and a little of the retained water (about 2-3 tablespoons) until smooth.
6. Transfer into a bowl. Add the remaining cashew pieces and mix.
7. Tastes great with whole grain bread or whole grain crackers.

Hummus

Ingredients:
- 1 can (14.5 ounce) chickpeas (garbanzo beans), unsalted, drain and retain the liquid, rinsed
- 2 - 3 teaspoons tahini (as per your taste)
- 2 cloves garlic, crushed
- 1/2 teaspoon sea salt or to taste
- 1 1/2 tablespoons fresh lemon juice
- 3 tablespoons extra virgin olive oil + extra for drizzling
- Pepper to taste
- 1/4 teaspoon paprika or to taste (optional)
- 1 tablespoon parsley (optional)

Method:
1. Blend together all the ingredients except olive oil, paprika and parsley along with 3-4 tablespoons of the retained liquid. With the food processor running, slowly pour olive oil and blend until smooth.
2. To serve, pour the hummus in a serving dish and garnish with paprika and parsley. Drizzle some olive oil too and serve.

Walnut Feta Cheese Dip

Ingredients:
- 2 cups walnuts, chopped
- 2 cups feta cheese, crumbled
- 2 cloves garlic, minced
- 4 teaspoons lemon juice
- 1/2 cup fresh parsley
- 2 teaspoons Spanish hot paprika
- A little olive oil to garnish
- 1 cup water
- 1/4 teaspoon salt
- 2 tablespoons fresh oregano, chopped + extra for garnishing

Method:
1. Blend together all the ingredients in a blender until the consistency you desire is achieved.
2. If you like it nutty, give short pulses else blend until smooth and creamy.
3. Transfer into a serving bowl. Drizzle some olive oil and garnish with fresh oregano leaves.

Guacamole

Ingredients:

- 2 avocadoes, peeled, seeded, mashed with a fork
- 2 small cloves garlic, minced or grated
- 2 tablespoons lime juice
- 1 tomato, diced
- 1 white onion, minced
- 1 teaspoon sea salt
- 1/2 cup fresh cilantro, finely chopped
- 2 jalapeno peppers, finely sliced
- 1/4 teaspoon black pepper powder or to taste

Method:

1. Mix together all the ingredients in a bowl.
2. Use as desired.

Lemon Ricotta Kale Dip

Ingredients:
- 2 bunches kale, discard hard stems and ribs, chopped
- 1 1/2 cups park skim ricotta cheese
- 8 cloves garlic, peeled
- 1 medium onion, sliced
- 3 tablespoons nutritional yeast
- Juice of 2 lemon
- Zest of a lemon, grated
- 1/2 teaspoon fine sea salt
- 1/4 teaspoon cayenne pepper or to taste

Method:
1. Place a large saucepan over medium heat. Add kale, onion, garlic and about 1/2 cup of water.
2. Cook until kale is very tender. Stir once in a while. If the moisture in the saucepan is dried up, then add a little more water.
3. Remove from heat. Let it cool slightly.
4. Transfer the vegetables to a blender. Add ricotta, nutritional yeast, lemon juice, lemon zest, salt and cayenne pepper.
5. Blend until smooth and creamy. Transfer into a serving bowl.
6. Serve with vegetable sticks like carrots, cucumbers etc. or with whole grain crackers.

Chipotle Chili Bean Dip

Ingredients:
- 3/4 cup chickpeas, cooked, drained, rinsed
- 3/4 cup unsalted black beans, cooked, drained, rinsed
- 1 tablespoon tahini
- 2 tablespoons extra virgin olive oil
- 2 small chipotle chilies in adobo sauce
- 1 clove garlic, peeled
- 1/4 teaspoon hot sauce or to taste
- 2 teaspoons lemon juice
- 1/2 teaspoon fine sea salt

Method:
1. Add all the ingredients to a food processor and pulse until coarse and well combined.
2. Tastes great with raw vegetable sticks, chips or whole-wheat pita bread.

Mayonnaise

Ingredients:

- 2 eggs, room temperature
- 1/4 cup lemon juice or vinegar of your choice
- ½ teaspoon salt or to taste
- 1 teaspoon dry mustard
- 2 cups light olive oil

Method:

1. Add egg, salt, mustard and lemon juice to the blender (you can use an immersion blender too). Blend until smooth.
2. With the blender running, slowly pour the olive oil in a thin stream. Blend until the consistency you desire is achieved.
3. Transfer into an airtight container and store in the refrigerator until use.

Chapter 7: Whole Food breakfast Recipes

Savory Sausage and Cheddar Breakfast Casserole

Ingredients:
- 2 1/2 cups sourdough or whole wheat bread cubes
- 4 eggs
- 1/2 cup spinach, roughly chopped
- 1 cup milk
- 1/2 cup cooked breakfast sausages
- 1/2 cup cheddar cheese, grated
- 2 cloves garlic, minced
- 1/4 teaspoon pepper powder
- 1/4 teaspoon salt or to taste
- 1/4 teaspoon dried sage

Method:
1. Grease a baking dish. Lay bread cubes at the bottom of the dish followed by sausages and finally spinach.
2. Add eggs, milk, garlic, salt, pepper and sage to a bowl and whisk well. Pour over the spinach layer.
3. Finally sprinkle with cheese.
4. Cover and refrigerate for at least 2-3 hours.
5. Remove from the refrigerator, uncover and bake in a preheated oven at 350 degree F for about 50 minutes or until the top is golden brown.
6. Remove from the oven and cool for about 10 minutes before serving.

Cauliflower Pancakes

Ingredients:
- 1 cup cauliflower florets
- 1 tablespoon flat leaf parsley, chopped
- 1 egg + extra eggs for serving
- 1/4 cup leek, cleaned, chopped
- 1/4 cup almond flour
- 1/4 cup smoked gouda cheese
- Salt to taste
- Pepper powder to taste
- 2-3 tablespoons coconut oil

Method:
1. Place cauliflower florets in the food processor bowl and pulse until you get a coarse and rice like texture. Transfer into a bowl.
2. Place a pan over medium heat. Add 1/2-tablespoon oil. When oil is heated, add leek and sauté until translucent.
3. Add garlic and sauté for a few seconds until fragrant. Remove from heat and transfer into the bowl of cauliflower.
4. Add parsley, salt, pepper, almond flour, and egg and Gouda cheese. Mix well.
5. Place a nonstick pan over medium heat. Add 1/2-teaspoon oil. When oil is heated, add about a spoonful of cauliflower mixture on the pan and spread a little using the back of a spoon.
6. Cook until the bottom side is golden brown. Flip sides and cook the other side too.

7. Remove on to a serving platter.
8. Repeat step 5 and 6 with the remaining batter.
9. Meanwhile, place another pan over medium heat. Add fry some eggs, sunny side up to serve. If you desire, flip sides and cook the other side too.
10. Remove on to the serving platter and serve.

Blueberry & Toasted Almond Muesli

Ingredients:
- 1 cup blueberries
- 1 cup skim milk
- 1 cup rolled oats
- 1/4 cups almonds, sliced, toasted

Method:
1. Add milk and oats to a bowl. Stir well. Cover and place in the refrigerator overnight.
2. Before serving, remove from the refrigerator.
3. Top it with blueberries. Garnish with almonds and serve.

Quinoa Breakfast Bowl

Ingredients:
- 2 eggs
- 1/2 cup cooked quinoa
- 1/2 cup tomatoes, chopped
- 1/2 cup onions, diced
- 1/2 cups spinach
- 1 teaspoon white vinegar
- 1/2 tablespoon Sriracha sauce
- 1/2 tablespoon coconut oil
- Salt to taste
- Pepper powder to taste

Method:
1. Place a skillet over medium heat. Add oil. When oil is heated, add onions and sauté until pink.
2. Add tomatoes and sauté for 4-5 minutes or until the tomatoes begin to mash.
3. Add spinach, salt and pepper and cook until spinach wilts.
4. Add quinoa and mix well. Remove the pan from heat.
5. Add Sriracha sauce. Mix well and transfer into 2 serving bowls
6. Place a pot of water over high heat and bring to a boil.
7. Lower heat and add vinegar. Break an egg into a bowl and slowly slide it into the simmering water.
8. When the egg is cooked, remove from the water and place over the quinoa mixture in the bowl.

9. Boil the other egg in the similar manner.
10. Serve immediately.

Green Egg Skillet Bake

Ingredients:
- 6 large eggs
- 1 large white onion, thinly sliced
- 6 cups collard greens, chopped
- 6 cups spinach, chopped
- 8 white mushrooms, sliced
- 6 cloves garlic, peeled, minced, divided
- 1 1/2 tablespoons olive oil
- 1 teaspoon red pepper flakes or to taste
- 1 teaspoon dried oregano
- 1 1/2 teaspoons ground cumin
- Freshly ground black pepper to taste
- Salt to taste
- 3 tablespoons Greek yogurt
- 4 teaspoons 1% milk or light coconut milk
- 3 teaspoons red chili paste
- Cooking spray

Method:
1. Place a heavy bottomed pot over medium high heat. Add oil. When oil is heated, add onion and sauté until onions turn light brown.
2. Add salt, pepper and collard greens and cook for a couple of minutes until it turns bright green.
3. Add half the garlic, cumin, oregano, red pepper and sauté for a few seconds.
4. Add spinach and cook until spinach wilts.
5. Remove from heat.

6. Spray a large cast iron skillet with cooking spray. Remove spinach mixture from the pot with a slotted spoon and add to the iron skillet.
7. Place mushrooms all over it. Make 6 cavities (big enough to fit an egg) in the spinach mixture. Crack an egg into each of the cavity. Sprinkle salt and pepper.
8. Place the skillet in a preheated oven and bake at 400 degree F until eggs are set.
9. Let it remain in the oven for 5 minutes.
10. Remove from oven and serve.

Scrambled Tofu

Ingredients:
- 2 tablespoons olive oil
- 2 bunches green onions, chopped
- 2 cans (14.5 ounce each) peeled, diced tomatoes along with the juice
- 2 packages (12 ounce each) firm silken tofu, drained, mashed
- 1/2 teaspoon ground turmeric
- Salt to taste
- Pepper powder to taste
- 1/2 teaspoon red chili flakes or to taste
- 1 green chili, sliced (optional)
- 1 cup cheddar cheese, shredded (optional)

Method:
1. Place a skillet over medium heat. Add oil. When the oil is heated, add green onions. Sauté until the green onions are tender.
2. Add turmeric, green chili, salt, and pepper. Sauté for a couple of minutes.
3. Add tofu and tomatoes along with the juice. Mix well.
4. Lower heat and let it heat thoroughly. Sprinkle cheddar cheese if using, and serve.

Grilled Vegetable Panzanella

Ingredients:
- 2 demi whole wheat baguette (about 6 inches long) sliced into 1/2 inch thick slices
- 1 green bell pepper quartered
- 1 red bell pepper quartered
- 2 medium yellow squash, cut into 1/4 inch thick rounds
- 2 medium zucchini, cut into 1/4 inch thick rounds
- 2 pint cherry tomatoes, halved, divided
- 4 cloves garlic, peeled
- 4 tablespoons balsamic vinegar
- 1/2 cup basil leaves + extra for garnishing, chopped
- 1 tablespoon fresh thyme leaves, chopped
- 1 tablespoon fresh oregano leaves, chopped

Method:
1. Preheat a grill or grill pan.
2. Grill the baguette slices, zucchini, squash and bell peppers for about 5 minutes per side.
3. Remove from the grill and keep it warm.
4. Blend together half the tomatoes, vinegar, garlic, oregano, thyme and basil until smooth. Transfer into a bowl and set aside.
5. Chop bread, zucchini, squash and bell pepper into about an inch size pieces. Transfer into a large bowl.
6. Add the remaining tomatoes and pour the blended tomato mixture over it.
7. Toss well, cover and set aside for at least 30 minutes.

8. Serve garnished with basil.

Chapter 8: Smoothies Recipes

Strawberry Almond Butter Smoothie

Ingredients:
- 16 ounces strawberries, chopped
- 4 tablespoons smooth almond butter
- 2 cups almond milk, unsweetened
- Ice cubes as desired

Method:
1. Place all the ingredients in a blender until smooth.
2. Pour into tall glasses and serve.

The 30 Day Whole Food Challenge

Rainbow Chard Ginger Fruit Smoothie

Ingredients:
- 12 ounces rainbow chard
- 2 cups frozen mango
- 2 inch pieces ginger, peeled, sliced
- 2 apples, cored, chopped
- 2 tablespoons chia seeds
- 1 1/2 cups water
- Ice cubes as desired

Method:
1. Place all the ingredients in a blender until smooth.
2. Pour into tall glasses and serve.

Pineapple Breeze Smoothie

Ingredients:
- 2 cups fresh pineapple, cubed
- 1 1/2 cups coconut milk
- 1 cup pineapple juice
- Ice cubes as desired

Method:
1. Place all the ingredients in a blender until smooth.
2. Pour into tall glasses and serve.

Kale n Berry Smoothie

Ingredients:
- 1 cup kale leaves, discard hard stems and ribs
- 2/3 cup strawberries
- 2/3 cup blueberries
- 2 medium bananas, peeled, sliced
- 3 cups almond milk
- 2 tablespoons chia seeds + extra for serving
- 2 tablespoons hemp powder
- 2 tablespoons ground flax seeds
- 2 tablespoons acai berry
- 2 teaspoons ground cinnamon
- Ice cubes as desired

Method:
1. Place all the ingredients in a blender and blend until smooth.
2. Pour into tall glasses.
3. Sprinkle chia seeds on top and serve.

Mixed Fruit Smoothie

Ingredients:
- 1 cup fresh or frozen blueberries
- 1 cup fresh or frozen strawberries
- 1 cup almond milk, unsweetened
- 1 cup apple juice or berry juice

Method:
1. Place all the ingredients in a blender and blend until smooth.
2. Pour into tall glasses and serve.
3. If you are using frozen strawberries and blueberries, then do not thaw.
4. Serve with crushed ice if you are using fresh fruits.

Fig Smoothie

Ingredients:
- 4 fresh figs, discard stem, quartered
- 12 strawberries, chopped
- 1 banana, peeled, sliced
- 2 cups coconut milk or almond milk
- 2 teaspoons honey
- 2 teaspoons ground cinnamon
- 2 tablespoons chia seeds + extra for garnishing
- Ice cubes as desired

Method:
1. Place all the ingredients in a blender and blend until smooth.
2. Pour into tall glasses.
3. Sprinkle chia seeds on top and serve.

Chapter 9: Whole Food Soup Recipes
Lentil soup

Ingredients:
- 1 cup yellow lentil
- 2 cups water
- 2 green chilies, slit
- Salt to taste
- 1 teaspoon turmeric powder
- 1 teaspoon fenugreek seeds
- 1 teaspoon sesame seeds
- 1 tablespoon oil
- Parsley leaves to sprinkle

Method:
1. Add the water to a pan and bring to a rolling boil.
2. Add in the yellow lentils and cook for 30 to 45 minutes or until soft.
3. Add the oil to a pan and toss in crushed fenugreek and sesame seeds.
4. Add the chilies and allow it to brown.
5. Toss this into the soup and stir until well combined.
6. Add salt and simmer for 5 minutes.
7. Serve hot with a sprinkling of parsley leaves.

Mushroom soup

Ingredients:
- 1 cup mushrooms, chopped
- 1 cup milk
- 1 tablespoon corn flour
- Salt to taste
- Pepper to taste
- 1 tablespoon dried oregano
- 1 tablespoon dried rosemary
- 1 tablespoon dried thyme
- Parsley leaves to sprinkle

Method:
1. Add the milk to a saucepan and bring to a boil.
2. Add in the chopped mushrooms and allow it to soften.
3. Add in the salt, pepper, oregano, rosemary and thyme and mix until well combined.
4. Add the corn flour to a small bowl and add in a little water to make a paste.
5. Add the paste to the soup and allow it to thicken.
6. Serve hot with a sprinkling of parsley leaves on top.

Golden Squash Curry Soup

Ingredients:
- 2 medium sized butternut squash, peeled, deseeded, cubed
- 2 large onions, chopped
- 2 inch piece fresh ginger, peeled, minced
- 6 cloves garlic, chopped
- 6 cups vegetable broth or chicken broth
- 12 ounce coconut milk
- 2 teaspoons curry powder
- 1 teaspoon turmeric powder
- 1/4 cup fresh cilantro, chopped
- 1 teaspoon salt or to taste
- 1/2 teaspoon white pepper powder or to taste
- 1 tablespoon olive oil

Method:
1. Take a large saucepan and place over medium heat. Add oil. When oil is heated, add onions and sauté until translucent.
2. Add turmeric powder, garlic, ginger and curry powder and sauté for a few seconds until fragrant. Add squash and broth and bring to a boil.
3. Lower heat, cover and simmer until the squash is tender. Remove from heat and cool slightly. Add coconut milk and blend with an immersion blender or blend in a blender until smooth.
4. Pour the soup back into the saucepan.

5. Reheat the soup. If you find the soup too thick, add some more broth, garnish with cilantro and serve.

Seafood Gazpacho

Ingredients:
- 1 pound bay scallops, rinsed, pat dried
- 1/2 pound shrimp, cooked, rinsed, pat dried
- 1 large yellow bell pepper, diced into 1/4 inch pieces
- 1 medium onion, minced
- 2 medium tomatoes, deseeded, chopped
- 1 1/3 cups cucumber, chopped
- 6 cloves garlic, peeled, pressed
- 4 tablespoons extra virgin olive oil
- 2 cans (4 ounce each) diced green chili
- 6 cups tomato juice
- Salt to taste
- Freshly cracked pepper to taste
- 1/2 cup lemon juice
- 1/2 cup fresh cilantro, chopped

Method:
1. Pour lemon juice over the scallops and set aside. If you don't like your scallops raw, then steam for just a minute and then marinate in lemon juice.
2. Add rest of the ingredients in a bowl and mix well. Let it sit for a while for the flavors to set in.
3. Add scallops to it. Mix well and chill for at least an hour.
4. Serve chilled in soup bowls.

Mexican Soup

Ingredients:
- 2 small zucchinis, chopped into 1/4 inch cubes
- 1 large green bell pepper, chopped into 1/4 inch pieces
- 2 medium onions, minced
- 2 cups collard greens, chopped
- 2 cups frozen yellow corn
- 2 cans (15 ounces each) diced tomatoes
- 2 cans (4 ounces each) diced green chili
- 4 cups black beans, rinsed
- 6 1/4 cups vegetable broth
- 1/2 cup pumpkin seeds
- 2 teaspoons chili powder or to taste
- 2 teaspoons ground cumin
- 2 teaspoons dried oregano
- 1 cup fresh cilantro, chopped
- Salt to taste
- Pepper powder to taste

Method:
1. Place a soup pot or large saucepan over medium. Add about 2 tablespoons of broth.
2. Add onions, garlic and bell pepper and sauté for about 5-6 minutes.
3. Add tomatoes, chili powder and mix again. Add remaining broth and simmer for 5 minutes.
4. Increase heat to high. Add beans, green chili, corn, cumin and oregano. Stir well and let it boil.

5. Lower heat to low, simmer for about 10 minutes.
6. Add zucchini, collard greens and simmer for another 5 minutes.
7. Add pumpkin seeds, cilantro, salt, and pepper. Stir well and remove from heat and serve immediately.

Tofu Noodle Soup

Ingredients:
- 9 cups ionized alkaline water
- 3 cups tofu, chopped
- 3 carrots, peeled, diced
- 1 1/2 cups fresh or frozen corn
- 1/2 cup parsley, chopped
- 5 stalks celery, chopped
- 10 tablespoons vegetarian broth powder
- 1 1/2 teaspoons sea salt or Himalayan salt
- 1 teaspoon pepper powder
- 3/4 box quinoa spaghetti noodles, broken into 2 inch strips

Method:
1. Add all the ingredients except noodles to a soup pot or large saucepan. Place the saucepan over medium heat. Bring to a boil.
2. Lower heat, cover and simmer until the vegetables are tender.
3. Add noodles and cook until the noodles are al dente.
4. Ladle into individual soup bowls and serve immediately

Kale Soup

Ingredients:
- 1 large onion, chopped
- 2 medium carrots, peeled, cubed
- 4 red potatoes, rinsed, scrubbed, cubed
- 6 cups kale, hard ribs and stems removed, finely sliced
- 4 stalks celery, chopped
- 10 cups vegetable stock
- 4 teaspoons dried sage
- 4 teaspoons dried thyme
- Salt to taste
- Pepper powder to taste

Method:
1. Place a large saucepan over medium heat. Add about a tablespoon of broth. Add onions and sauté until onions are translucent. Add garlic and sauté for a couple of minutes.
2. Add remaining broth, carrots, potatoes, celery, sage, thyme, salt and pepper and bring to a boil.
3. Lower heat, cover and cook until tender.
4. Add kale and cook until kale wilts and serve immediately.

Thai Chicken Soup

Ingredients:
- 1/2 tablespoon coconut oil
- 2 shallots, chopped
- 1/4 cup cilantro, chopped
- 2 cups chicken stock
- 14 ounces coconut milk
- 1/2 tablespoon honey or agave nectar
- 1/2 head broccoli
- ¼ pound crimini mushrooms
- 1 1/2 tablespoons fresh lime juice
- 1/2 pound chicken breasts (skinless-boneless) cut into small pieces
- 2 teaspoons Thai red curry paste or to taste
- 1 1/2 tablespoons fish sauce
- 1/2 cup cilantro, minced
- 2 Serrano chilies, thinly sliced
- 1/4 cup scallions
- 1 lime, cut into wedges

Method:
1. Place a large soup pot or saucepan over medium heat. Add oil.
2. When the oil is heated, add shallots and cilantro, sauté for a couple of minutes.
3. Add stock, coconut milk, and agave nectar and reduce heat.
4. Simmer for about 10 minutes.

5. Strain the broth. Retain the broth and discard the shallots and cilantro.
6. Pour the broth to saucepan. Keep on medium heat.
7. Add mushrooms, chicken, and broccoli and cook until tender.
8. Add the curry paste, fish sauce and lime juice. Stir well.
9. Serve in soup bowls garnished with scallions, cilantro, chilies, and lime wedges.

French Onion Soup

Ingredients:
- 3 medium sweet onions, halved, thinly sliced
- 1 can (14.5 ounce) chicken broth
- 1 can (14.5 ounce) beef broth
- 1 tablespoon parmesan cheese, shredded
- 1 tablespoon Romano cheese, shredded
- 4 slices thin provolone cheese
- 4 slices thin Swiss cheese
- 1 tablespoon olive oil
- 1/2 teaspoon dry sherry (optional)

Method:
1. Place a large soup pot or saucepan over medium heat. Add oil. When oil is heated, add onions and sauté until the onions are golden brown.
2. Add beef and chicken broth. Bring to a boil. Add sherry and remove from heat.
3. Divide the soup into ovenproof soup bowls. Place the bowls in a baking pan. Sprinkle cheese into each of the crocks.
4. Add provolone cheese slices and Swiss slices to each of the bowls.
5. Place the baking pan along with the bowls in the oven. Place it close to the heating element.
6. Broil for a while until the cheese is golden brown.
7. Remove from the oven and serve after 5 minutes.

Beef Stew

Ingredients:
- 3/4 pound beef stew meat
- 4 ounce mushrooms, sliced
- 1 medium sweet potato, peeled, rinsed, chopped into chunks
- 1 medium onion, chopped
- 1 stalk celery, chopped
- 1 1/2 tablespoons garlic, minced
- 1 tablespoon coconut oil
- 1 tablespoon butter
- 1 bay leaf
- 3 cups beef broth
- 1/2 teaspoon garlic powder
- 1 tablespoon arrowroot powder
- 1/2 tablespoon balsamic vinegar
- Salt to taste
- Pepper powder to taste

Method:
1. Place a large Dutch oven or saucepan over medium heat. Add coconut oil. When oil melts, add onions and garlic and sauté until onions are translucent.
2. Sprinkle garlic powder, salt and pepper over meat. Coat it well.
3. Meanwhile, place a skillet over medium heat. Add 1/2-tablespoon butter. When butter melts, add meat

and cook on both the sides for about a minute each. Remove from the skillet and add it to the Dutch oven.
4. Add 2 cups beef broth and reduce heat to low.
5. Add sweet potatoes, celery and bay leaf and stir. Let it simmer.
6. Meanwhile, add remaining butter to the skillet. Add mushrooms and sauté until mushrooms are tender. Add vinegar.
7. Add arrowroot powder to the remaining beef broth. Add this to the pan of mushrooms stirring constantly until thick. Transfer into the Dutch oven. Mix well and simmer for about an hour or until the meat is cooked.
8. Ladle the stew into bowls and serve.

Chapter 10: Whole foods Salad Recipes

Rainbow Soba Salad

Ingredients:
- 1 cup green cabbage, shredded
- 2 kale leaves, discard hard stems and ribs, finely sliced
- 1/2 cup red cabbage, shredded
- 3/4 tablespoon low sodium tamari
- 1 tablespoon rice vinegar
- 1/2 tablespoon honey
- 2 tablespoons sesame seeds, toasted
- 4 ounces buckwheat soba noodles, cook according to instructions on the package

Method:
1. To make dressing: Add vinegar, tamari and honey to a bowl and whisk well.
2. Add all the vegetables to a bowl. Pour the dressing over it. Toss well and keep it aside.
3. Just before serving. Add noodles and toss well.
4. Sprinkle sesame seeds and serve.

Arugula, Grape, and Sunflower Seed Salad

Ingredients:
- 1 cup red grapes, halved
- 5 cups baby arugula, loosely packed
- 2 tablespoons sunflower seeds, toasted
- 1 teaspoon fresh thyme, chopped

For dressing:
- 1 1/2 tablespoons red wine vinegar
- 1 teaspoon honey or maple syrup
- 1 teaspoon olive oil
- 1/4 teaspoon ground mustard
- 1/8 teaspoon salt
- 1/8 teaspoon pepper powder

Method:
1. To make dressing: Add all the ingredients for dressing to a small bowl and whisk well.
2. Mix together salad ingredients in a bowl and toss well.
3. Pour dressing over salad, toss again and serve.

Mango Quinoa Salad

Ingredients:
- 1/2 cup quinoa, rinsed
- 1 cup water
- 1 small mango, peeled, deseeded, chopped
- 1 cup corn kernels
- 1 1/2 tablespoons chives, finely chopped
- 1/4 teaspoon lemon zest, grated
- 1 tablespoon lemon juice

Method:
1. Place a saucepan over medium heat. Add quinoa and water and bring to a boil.
2. Lower heat, cover and simmer until all the water dries up. Remove from heat and uncover after 5 minutes. Using a fork, fluff the quinoa. Transfer into a bowl.
3. Add rest of the ingredients, toss well and serve.

Black Beans and Corn Salad

Ingredients:
- 1 1/2 cups black beans, cooked
- 1 cup corn
- 1/2 cup cherry tomatoes, halved
- 1 green onion, sliced
- 1/2 a red pepper, chopped
- 1/4 teaspoon ground cumin
- 1/4 teaspoon garlic powder
- 1/2 avocado, peeled, sliced
- 1/4 teaspoon avocado oil
- 2 tablespoons lime juice
- 1/2 teaspoon salt or to taste

Method:
1. Add all the ingredients to a bowl, toss well and serve.

Caper and Lemon Salad

Ingredients:

- 3 pounds salmon fillet
- Juice of a lemon or to taste
- 1 teaspoon lemon zest, grated
- 1/3 cup canned capers, drained, rinsed
- 3 stalks celery, chopped
- 2 tablespoons fresh dill, chopped
- 3 tablespoons extra virgin olive oil
- Salt to taste
- Pepper to taste

Method:

1. Place salmon in a baking dish. Season the salmon with salt and pepper and bake in a preheated oven at 350 degree F for 10 minutes or until the salmon is flaky when pierced with a fork.
2. Transfer the salmon to a serving bowl. Add rest of the ingredients and toss well.
3. Place in the refrigerator until use.

Summer Salad

Ingredients:
- 1 cup cooked chick peas, drained, rinsed
- A handful basil leaves, chopped
- 1 cup cherry tomatoes, sliced
- 1 cucumber, chopped
- 1 clove garlic, minced
- 1 tablespoon olive oil
- 1 tablespoon lemon juice
- Salt to taste

Method:
1. Add all the ingredients to a bowl, toss well and refrigerate for at least an hour before serving.

Caribbean Chicken Salad

Ingredients:
- 1 chicken breast half, skinless, boneless
- 1 medium onion, chopped
- 1 tomato, deseeded, chopped
- 1/2 pound mixed salad greens
- 1 teaspoon jalapeno pepper, minced
- A handful of cilantro, chopped
- 1/2 cup pineapple chunks, drained
- 2 tablespoons teriyaki marinade sauce
- 2 cups corn tortilla chips to serve, broken into large pieces

For dressing:
- 2 tablespoons Dijon mustard
- 2 teaspoons sugar
- 2 teaspoons apple cider
- 1/2 tablespoon olive oil
- 1 teaspoon lime juice
- 2 tablespoons honey

Method:
1. Place chicken breast in a bowl and pour teriyaki marinade sauce. Toss well and refrigerate for a minimum of 2 hours.
2. Mix together in a bowl tomatoes, onion, jalapeno pepper and cilantro and refrigerate until use.

3. For dressing: Mix together all the ingredients for dressing and whisk well. Cover and refrigerate until use.
4. Remove the marinated chicken from the refrigerator and grill on a preheated grill for about 6-8 minutes per side over high heat. Discard the marinade.
5. When done, remove from the grill. When cool enough to handle, cut the grilled chicken into strips.
6. To arrange salad: Place salad greens on a serving plate. Pour the tomato mixture over the greens. Layer with pineapple chunks.
7. Sprinkle tortilla chips over the pineapple layer. Lay the chicken strips next.
8. Finally pour the dressing all over and serve.
9. You can also arrange in the similar manner on individual serving plates.

Detox Salad

Ingredients:
- 1 cup carrots, shredded
- 1 head broccoli, stems removed, broken into florets
- 1 small head cauliflower, stems removed, broken into florets
- 1/2 cup currants
- 1/4 cup raisins
- 1/4 cup sunflower seeds
- 1/4 cup fresh parsley, finely chopped
- Kelp granules to taste (optional)
- Pure maple syrup to serve
- Salt to taste
- Pepper powder to taste

Method:
1. Add cauliflower and broccoli to the food processor and process until fine. Transfer into a large bowl.
2. Add rest of the ingredients to the bowl of broccoli and toss well.
3. Taste and adjust the seasonings if necessary.
4. Drizzle maple syrup and serve.

Chapter 11: Whole Foods Snack Recipes
Roast potatoes in mint gravy

Ingredients:
- 2 large potatoes
- 1 red onion
- 1 bell pepper
- ½ cup mint leaves
- 2 tablespoons Indian curry powder (Garam masala)
- 2 cups coconut milk
- Salt to taste
- Red chili to taste
- 5 tablespoons oil
- Mint to sprinkle

Method:
1. Chop the potatoes, onion and bell pepper into squares.
2. Add the oil to a pan and toss into the vegetables to roast them thoroughly.
3. Add the coconut milk and mint to a blender and make a smooth paste.
4. Add to a pan along with the curry powder, salt, red chili powder and bring to a boil.
5. Toss in the vegetables and cook until soft.
6. Serve with a sprinkling of fresh mint leaves on top.

Steamed samosas

Ingredients:
- 1 cup whole wheat flour
- ¼ cup water
- 1 carrot, chopped
- ½ cup beans, chopped
- 1/4 cabbage, chopped
- 1 cup green peas
- 1 large potato, chopped
- 1 tablespoon Indian curry powder (Garam Masala)
- Salt to taste
- Chili powder to taste
- 1 tablespoon oil

Method:
1. Chop all the vegetables into tiny pieces.
2. Add the oil to a pan and toss in all the vegetables.
3. Cook until soft and add in the salt, Garam masala, chili powder and salt and mix until well combined.
4. Add the flour to a bowl and add in the water to make dough.
5. Make small roundlets out of the dough and roll them out into small circles.
6. Place a tablespoon of the vegetable mix in the center and close the ball into a triangle shape.
7. Steam for 15 to 20 minutes or until soft.
8. Serve with a dip of your choice.

Spicy chicken patties

Ingredients:
- 2 cup chicken meat, any cut
- ½ cup whole wheat flour
- ½ cup semolina
- 2 tablespoons Indian curry powder (Garam masala)
- 1 tablespoon fenugreek leaves
- 1 teaspoon turmeric powder
- 1 teaspoon cumin powder
- 1 teaspoon coriander powder
- 1/4 cup Greek yogurt
- Salt to taste
- Red chili powder to taste
- Mint leaves to sprinkle
- 5 tablespoons vegetable oil

Method:
1. Add the chicken meat to a bowl along with the curry powder, fenugreek leaves, turmeric powder, cumin powder, coriander powder, salt and chili powder and mix until well combined.
2. You can add in a little Greek yogurt to bind the ingredients together.
3. Set aside for 30 minutes.
4. Add the wheat four to a bowl along with the yogurt and mix to form a semi-thick batter.
5. Add the oil to a pan and allow it to heat.
6. Place the semolina on a plate.

7. Make small roundlets from the chicken mix and flatten it by placing between your palms.
8. Dip it in the wheat batter and coat it with the semolina before placing on the hot oil.
9. Allow it to brown on one side before flipping it over.
10. Serve hot with a sprinkling of mint leaves on top.

Chickpea stuffed flat bread

Ingredients:
- 1 can chickpeas, drained
- 1 cup whole wheat flour
- ¼ cup water
- Salt to taste
- 1 lemon, juiced
- Red chili powder or paprika to taste
- 1 tablespoon cumin seeds
- Mint leaves to sprinkle
- Toasted sesame seeds to sprinkle

Method:
1. Drain the chickpeas and add to a blender along with the cumin seeds and make a smooth paste.
2. You can add in a little of its water if you like.
3. Add to a bowl along with the lemon juice, chili powder and salt and mix until well combined.
4. Add the wheat flour a bowl along with the water and make a firm dough.
5. All the dough to rest for 5 to 10 minutes.
6. Meanwhile, make small roundlets out of the chickpea mixture.
7. Now make equal number of roundlets out of the dough and flatten it out using a rolling pin.
8. Place one chickpea roundlet in the center of each and bring in the sides together to join at the top.
9. Roll it out again into the desired size.
10. Heat a griddle and add a little vegetable oil.

11. Roast the bread on both sides and serve hot with a sprinkling of mint leaves and toasted sesame seeds on top.

Spicy Pumpkin Seeds / Nuts

Ingredients:
- 6 cups raw pumpkin seeds (pepitas)
- 4 tablespoons butter or ghee, melted
- 2 teaspoons cayenne pepper
- 2 teaspoons chili powder (optional)
- Sea salt to taste

Method:
1. Place the pepitas in a baking dish. Add ghee, cayenne pepper, chili powder, sea salt and cayenne pepper and toss well.
2. Bake in a preheated oven at 350 degree F for about 10 minutes or until done. Cool and store in an airtight container in the refrigerator.

Note: You can also make spicy nuts using the same ingredients. You replace pumpkin seeds with nuts of your choice like almonds, macadamia etc.

Apple Sandwiches with Granola and Peanut Butter

Ingredients:
- 3 small apples, cored, cut horizontally into 1/2 inch thick rounds
- 5 tablespoons peanut butter
- 2 teaspoons lemon juice (optional)
- 3 tablespoons semisweet chocolate chips
- 5 tablespoons granola

Method:
1. Take half of the apple slices and apply peanut butter on one side of the slice.
2. Sprinkle chocolate chips and granola over these buttered slices.
3. Cover with the remaining half of apple slices to complete the sandwiches.
4. Place on a serving platter and serve.

Note: you can replace peanut butter with almond butter.

Kale Chips/Zucchini

Ingredients:
- 2-3 bunches of kale leaves, discard hard stem and ribs, rinsed, drained, dried, torn
- Cooking spray
- Salt to taste
- Red chili flakes to taste (optional)

Method:
1. Sprinkle salt and chili on kale. Spray with cooking spray. Keep aside for a while.
2. Spread the leaves on a baking sheet.
3. Bake in a preheated oven at 250 degree F or until crisp and done.

Note: You can make zucchini chips in similar manner by replacing kale leaves with thin slices of zucchini.

Cucumber Boats

Ingredients:
- 2 cucumbers, peeled, cut into 2 lengthwise, deseeded
- 5-6 tablespoons hummus - refer chapter 1
- 8 baby tomatoes, sliced
- A handful of arugula
- 1 carrot, shredded
- Pepper powder to taste
- Salt to taste

Method:
1. Spread hummus on the inside of the cucumber boats. Spread arugula, carrots and tomatoes over it.
2. Season with salt and pepper and serve.

Crispy Edamame Popcorn

Ingredients:
- 6 ounces frozen edamame, shelled, thawed
- 1 teaspoon lemon juice
- 1 teaspoon olive oil
- Salt to taste

Method:
1. Place edamame in a bowl. Add oil and lemon juice.
2. Place in a foil lined baking sheet and bake in a preheated oven at 375 degree F for about 45 minutes or until light brown and crisp.
3. Remove from oven and sprinkle salt immediately. Cool completely and store in an airtight container.

Almond Butter Energy Balls

Ingredients:
- 1/2 cup sesame seeds, toasted
- 1/2 cup sunflower seeds
- 1/2 cup raisins
- 1 cup almond butter
- 1/2 cup chocolate chips
- 1/4 cup cocoa
- 1/2 cup dried cranberries
- 1/2 cup rolled oats
- 1/4 cup honey + extra if required
- 3/4 cup nuts of your choice, chopped

Method:
1. Add all the ingredients except nuts to a bowl and mix well. . If your mixture is not sticky, add some more honey and mix well.
2. Divide the mixture and shape into 10 small balls. Roll the balls in the nuts and serve.

Blueberry Basil Muffins

Ingredients:
- 3 1/3 cups sprouted whole wheat flour
- 2/3 cup blue cornmeal
- 1 cup butter, unsalted, melted + extra from greasing
- 4 large eggs
- 2 cups milk
- 1 1/3 cups honey
- 1 teaspoon baking soda
- 3 teaspoons baking powder
- 1 teaspoon ground cinnamon
- 1 teaspoon salt
- 4 teaspoons lemon zest, grated
- 1/2 cup basil, finely chopped
- 2 heaping cups blueberries

Method:
1. Mix together all the dry ingredients in a large bowl and set aside.
2. Whisk together butter, honey, milk and eggs in another bowl. Pour this mixture into the bowl of dry ingredients and stir.
3. Add blueberries, basil, and lemon zest and mix well.
4. Grease 24 muffin tins with a little melted butter. Pour batter in the muffin tins. Fill up to only 2/3 the tin.
5. Bake in a preheated oven at 400 degree F for about 20 minutes or until a toothpick when inserted in the center of the muffin comes out clean.

6. Remove from the oven and cool for 5 minutes.
7. Run a knife around the edges of the muffin and remove the muffins and place on a wire rack.
8. Serve warm or cold.

Pita Pizza

Ingredients:

For Pizza:
- 2 whole wheat pita breads (7 1/2 inches each)
- 1 1/2 ounces mozzarella cheese, grated
- 1/2 a yellow bell pepper, deseeded, chop into thin strips

For tomato sauce:
- 1 small yellow onion, peeled, chopped into 1 cm pieces
- 1 small bay leaf
- 7 ounces canned whole tomatoes, peeled, chopped
- 1/2 teaspoon olive oil
- 1 clove garlic, peeled, minced
- 1/4 teaspoon dried basil
- 1/4 teaspoon dried oregano
- 1/4 teaspoon crushed red pepper flakes
- 2 tablespoons tomato paste

Method:
1. To make tomato sauce: Place a pan over medium heat. Add oil. When oil is heated, add onion and garlic and sauté until brown.
2. Add oregano, basil, bay leaf, red pepper flakes, tomatoes and tomato paste.
3. Mix well and bring to a boil.

4. Lower heat to medium low and let it simmer for a while until the liquid is dried up.
5. Place pita bread on a baking sheet. Divide and spread tomato sauce over it. Sprinkle bell pepper strips followed by mozzarella cheese.
6. Bake in a preheated oven at 350 degree F for about 20 minutes or until the cheese melts.
7. Remove the pizzas from the oven and transfer on to your work area. Garnish with basil and cut each pizza into 12 wedges and serve.

Chapter 12: Whole Foods Main Course - Meat Recipes
Curried Chicken Over Spinach

Ingredients:
- 2 chicken breasts, boneless, skinless, chopped into bite sized pieces
- 1 small onion, halved, sliced
- 1 cup chicken stock
- 1 small red bell pepper, thinly sliced
- 3 bunches fresh spinach, rinsed
- 1/2 tablespoons fresh ginger, minced
- 2 cloves garlic, sliced
- 1 teaspoon curry powder
- 1/4 teaspoon turmeric powder
- 6 tablespoons coconut milk
- White pepper powder to taste
- Salt to taste

Method:
1. Boil a pot of water and spinach to it Boil for a minute and drain. Press to squeeze out the excess moisture. Sprinkle salt and pepper and set aside.
2. Place a nonstick pan over medium low heat. Add onions and sauté for 5 minutes.
3. Add ginger and garlic and sauté for a couple of minutes until fragrant.
4. Add turmeric and curry powder and sauté,

5. Add stock, chicken, coconut milk and simmer for 5-6 minutes. Add bell pepper and cook until the chicken in tender.
6. To serve: Place blanched spinach on serving plates and place chicken mixture over it.

The 30 Day Whole Food Challenge

Chicken Kebabs with Tomato-Parsley Salad

Ingredients:
- 8 chicken breast halves, skinless, boneless, cut into 1 1/2 inch cubes
- 2 1/2 cups cherry tomatoes, chopped
- 4 cups fresh parsley leaves
- 6 tablespoons fresh lemon juice, divided
- 6 tablespoons extra virgin olive oil, divided
- 3 teaspoons dried oregano, divided
- 2 tablespoons garlic, minced, divided
- 1 1/2 teaspoons freshly ground black pepper powder, divided
- 1 1/2 teaspoons kosher salt, divided

Method:
1. Whisk together in a large bowl, 4 tablespoons lemon juice, 4 teaspoons garlic, 2 teaspoons oregano, 1-teaspoon salt, and 1-teaspoon pepper.
2. Add 2 tablespoons oil and whisk again. Add chicken and mix well. Cover and refrigerate for 2-3 hours.
3. Remove the chicken from the bowl and discard the marinade.
4. Fix chicken pieces on skewers.
5. Grill the chicken for about 6-7 minutes over high heat on a preheated grill. Turn the skewers a couple of times in between until chicken is cooked.
6. Mix together all the remaining ingredients and toss. Divide and place salad over individual serving plates.
7. Place chicken kebabs over the salad and serve.

Grilled Salmon and Lemon with Herbs

Ingredients:
- 1 1/4 pound salmon, remove skin on one side and pin bones
- 2 lemons halved
- 2 teaspoons extra virgin olive oil + extra for grilling
- 1/4 teaspoon black pepper powder
- 1/4 teaspoon fine sea salt
- 1-tablespoon fresh herbs chopped of your choice. You can also mix and chop.

Method:
1. Grease the grill grates and preheat the grill to medium high heat.
2. Apply oil over salmon and season with salt and pepper.
3. Place the salmon with its skin side down on the grill and cook until golden brown. Flip sides and cook the other side too.
4. Simultaneously, place lemon halves over the grill with its cut side down and grill until golden brown.
5. Remove salmon and lemons from the grill and place on a serving platter. Sprinkle fresh herbs and serve with grilled lemons.

Curried Shrimp

Ingredients:
- 2 pounds large shrimp, peeled
- 2 medium onions, chopped
- 8 cloves garlic, sliced
- 4 teaspoons ginger, minced
- 1 cup tomatoes, pureed
- 1 teaspoon ground turmeric
- 1 teaspoon ground cumin
- 1 teaspoon ground coriander
- 2 bunches fresh cilantro, minced
- 1/3 cup lime juice
- 4 tablespoons olive oil

Method:
1. Place a large saucepan over medium heat. Add oil. When oil is heated, add onions and garlic and sauté until onions are translucent.
2. Add tomatoes, ginger, cumin, coriander, and turmeric and mix well.
3. Lower heat and simmer for 5-6 minutes. Add shrimp and cook until done. Add cilantro and stir.
4. Remove from heat. Add lime juice and mix. Serve immediately.

Coconut Red Pork Curry

Ingredients:
- 1 1/2 pounds pork tenderloin
- 1 cup coconut milk
- 3 tablespoons canola oil
- 1 1/2 cups vegetable broth
- 1 1/2 tablespoons mild curry powder
- 3 tablespoons basil, chopped
- 1/2 package frozen haricots verts, cook according to instructions on the package
- Salt to taste

Method:
1. Mix together 1 tablespoon curry powder and 1 1/2 tablespoons oil and rub it on to pork tenderloin
2. Place an ovenproof skillet over high heat. Add remaining oil. When oil is heated, add pork and cook until brown on all the sides.
3. Remove from heat and place the skillet in a preheated oven and bake at 350 degree F for about 15 minutes or until a thermometer when inserted in the center of the tenderloin shows 155 degree F.
4. Remove the dish from the oven and cool. When cool enough to handle, slice into thin slices
5. Pour a little coconut milk and curry powder to a saucepan and blend until smooth.
6. Add rest of the coconut milk and vegetable broth and place the saucepan over medium heat and simmer until the mixture is slightly thick.
7. Add basil and mix. Remove from heat.

8. To serve: Arrange haricots verts over individual serving plates. Place pork slices over it. Pour sauce over pork and serve.

Grilled Teriyaki Pork Lettuce Wraps

Ingredients:
- 1 pork tenderloin of about 2 pounds
- 2 heads Boston Lettuce, separate leaves, rinse, pat dry
- 2/3 cup teriyaki sauce + extra for serving
- 1 cup carrots, peeled, shredded
- 1 cup radish, shredded
- 1 cup cucumber, shredded
- 1 cup Napa cabbage, shredded
- 1 cup mixed fresh herbs of your choice, chopped

Method:
1. Place pork in a bowl and pour teriyaki sauce over it. Coat well and marinate for at least a couple of hours in the refrigerator.
2. Preheat a grill to medium high. Carefully remove the pork from the bowl discarding the remaining marinade and place on the grill.
3. Grill until brown and done. Turn pork on and off. If you think that the pork is getting brown and not getting cooked inside, then push the pork to a comparatively cooler part of the grill.
4. When done, place the pork on your cutting board. When cool enough to handle, slice it into thin strips.
5. Place lettuce leaves on individual serving plates.
6. Sprinkle vegetables over the leaves. Place pork strips over it. Sprinkle mixed herbs. Drizzle some teriyaki sauce over it and serve.

The 30 Day Whole Food Challenge

Healthy Turkey Meatloaf

Ingredients:
- 1 1/2 cups baby spinach
- 1 small onion, quartered
- 1 stalk celery, roughly chopped
- 1 medium carrot, roughly chopped
- 3/4 pound ground lean turkey
- 1/2 tablespoon chia seeds that are soaked in 2-3 tablespoons water for 12-15 minutes
- 3/4 cup cooked quinoa, cooled
- 2 cloves garlic
- 1 1/2 tablespoons low sodium soy sauce
- 2 tablespoons barbeque sauce
- 1/4 teaspoon ground black pepper powder

Method:
1. Add onion, carrot, garlic, and celery to a food processor
2. Pulse it till its chopped finely.
3. Add the spinach and pulse it again for a couple of times. Transfer into a skillet.
4. Place the skillet over medium heat and cook until vegetables turn brown and liquid in the vegetables dries up.
5. Remove from heat and place in a large bowl.
6. When cool enough to handle, add chia seeds, ground turkey, quinoa, soy sauce and pepper and mix with your hands until well combined.
7. Line a baking sheet with parchment paper. Transfer meat mixture on to the baking sheet.

8. Shape into a loaf. Spread barbeque sauce on the top portion of the loaf.
9. Bake in a preheated oven at 425 degree F for about 40 minutes or brown and cooked well inside.
10. Remove from oven. Cool for a while and serve.

Rosemary Lamb Chops

Ingredients:
- 6 lamb chops
- 2 cloves garlic, pressed
- 3 tablespoons lemon juice
- Salt to taste
- Black pepper powder to taste
- 2 tablespoons fresh rosemary, chopped

Method:
1. Press garlic and set aside for a few minutes.
2. Add lemon juice, rosemary, garlic, salt and pepper to a bowl and mix well. Rub this mixture over the lamb chops and set aside.
3. Place an ovenproof cast iron skillet about 6-7 inches from the heat element in a broiler and let it heat for about 10 minutes.
4. Place lamb chops in the broiler and broil for about 5 minutes or until done.
5. Serve hot.

Beef Taco Pizza

Ingredients:
- 1 pound ground beef
- 1 1/2 cups unsalted black beans or pinto beans, cooked, drained, rinsed
- 1 1/2 cups corn kernels
- 2 pounds whole wheat pizza dough
- 1 1/2 cups hot salsa
- 1 1/2 cups mild cheddar cheese

Method:
1. Place a large skillet over medium heat. Add beef and cook until brown. Add corn, chili powder and beans and heat thoroughly.
2. Divide the pizza dough and roll out into a thin pizza.
3. Spread the beef mixture over it. Sprinkle cheese.
4. Bake in a preheated oven at 450 degree F until done.
5. Cut into wedges and serve.

Chapter 13: Whole Foods Vegetarian Recipes
Mushroom Stroganoff

Ingredients:
- 3/4 pound assorted mushrooms, thickly sliced
- 1/3 cup raw cashews
- 1 1/2 cups mushroom broth or vegetable broth
- 2 shallots, thinly sliced
- 1 teaspoon red wine vinegar
- 1/2 tablespoon paprika
- 1/2 teaspoon Dijon mustard
- 1/4 teaspoon ground black pepper
- 2 tablespoons fresh parsley or dill to garnish
- Fine sea salt to taste

Method:
1. Cover cashews with boiling water. Cover and set aside for 30 minutes.
2. Blend cashew along with 2 tablespoons water (discard the remaining water), vinegar and salt until smooth and creamy.
3. Place a heavy skillet over medium heat. Add mushrooms and shallots and cook with a little broth until mushrooms turn light brown. Add broth if necessary until the mushrooms are cooked.
4. Add remaining broth, mustard, paprika and pepper and bring to a boil.
5. Lower heat and simmer until sauce is thickened.
6. Add half the cashew cream and mix well.

7. Garnish with parsley and serve along with remaining cashew cream.

Spicy Black Bean Burrito

Ingredients:
- 4 whole wheat tortillas
- 1 red onion, chopped
- 4 cups canned black beans, rinsed, drained
- 2 red bell pepper, chopped
- 4 ounce low fat cheese
- 4 tablespoons extra virgin olive oil
- 1/4 teaspoon cayenne pepper
- 2 teaspoons chili powder or to taste
- Salt to taste
- Pepper powder to taste
- 1 tablespoon vegetable broth

Method:
1. Place a nonstick skillet over medium heat. Add onions, bell pepper and broth and cook for 4-5 minutes.
2. Add garlic, beans, olive oil, chili powder, cayenne pepper, salt and pepper. Heat thoroughly.
3. Lay the tortillas on your work area. Spread some of the mixture over it. Sprinkle cheese. Wrap and serve with salsa.

Asian Sautéed Cauliflower

Ingredients:
- 2 medium heads cauliflower, trimmed, cut into big pieces
- 4 tablespoons soy sauce
- 4 tablespoons rice vinegar or lemon juice
- 10 tablespoons vegetable broth
- 4 cloves garlic, pressed
- 1 teaspoon fresh ginger, grated
- 2 tablespoons extra virgin olive oil
- 2 tablespoons honey
- 1 fresh cilantro, chopped
- Salt to taste
- White pepper powder to taste
- 1 tablespoon dry mustard

Method:
1. Place a skillet over medium heat. Add 2 tablespoons broth and cauliflower, cover and cook for 5 minutes.
2. Mix together rest of the ingredients and add to cauliflower. Mix well and remove from heat.
3. Cover and set aside for a few minutes before serving.

Herbed Potatoes

Ingredients:
- 6 medium red potatoes, rinsed, cut into bite sized pieces
- 2 large cloves garlic, pressed
- 2 tablespoons fresh parsley, chopped
- 2 tablespoons fresh oregano, chopped
- 4 tablespoons extra virgin olive oil
- 2 tablespoons fresh lemon juice
- 2 teaspoons fresh rosemary, chopped
- Salt to taste
- Freshly cracked pepper to taste

Method:
1. Add a little salt to water in a steamer and bring to a boil.
2. Place potatoes in the steamer and cook until tender.
3. Mix together rest of the ingredients and add to the steamed potatoes. Toss well and serve.

Spinach Hummus Pinwheel Wraps

Ingredients:
- 2 whole grain tortillas
- 2 cups packed spinach, steamed
- 1 small red bell pepper, thinly sliced
- A few thin cucumber slices
- 1 clove garlic, peeled
- 1/2 a 15 ounce can unsalted cannellini beans
- 1/2 avocado, peeled, pitted, thinly sliced
- 2 tablespoons low sodium vegetable broth or water
- 1 tablespoon tahini
- 1 tablespoon lemon juice
- 1/4 teaspoon salt or to taste

Method:
1. To make spinach hummus: Add spinach, beans, lemon juice, tahini, garlic and salt to a food processor and pulse until smooth.
2. Place tortilla on your work area. Apply spinach hummus over it. Lay avocado, cucumber and bell pepper slices. Roll tightly and set-aside until use.
3. To serve, chop into 3/4-inch pinwheels and serve.

Chapter 14: Whole Food Sandwich Recipes
Cuban Sandwich

Ingredients:
- 2 whole grain mini baguettes, sliced open, halved
- Mayonnaise as required
- Dijon mustard (optional) as required
- 8 thin slices nitrate free lean deli ham
- 8 thin slices Swiss cheese
- 8 thin slices nitrate free deli salami
- 8 thin slices nitrate free deli smoked peppered turkey breast
- 1 cup baby spinach
- 2 large pickled dill, sliced
- 4 thin slices red onion
- 4 slices red bell pepper

Method:
1. Apply mayonnaise and mustard over each of the bread piece.
2. Place 2 slices each of ham, turkey, salami and Swiss cheese on to 4 pieces of bread.
3. Place a layer of pickle, spinach, onion and red pepper. Cover with remaining 4 pieces of bread to complete the sandwiches.
4. Grill in a sandwich maker and serve hot.

Turkey Sandwich

Ingredients:
- 4 slices whole wheat bread
- 4 slices turkey
- 6 slices tomatoes
- Hummus as required
- A handful of baby spinach

Method:
1. Spread hummus over bread slices.
2. Layer turkey, spinach and tomatoes over 2 slices of bread.
3. Cover with the remaining 2 slices of bread. Cut into desired shape and serve.

Open Face Apple Tahini Sandwich

Ingredients:
- 4 slices whole wheat or multigrain bread
- 2 tablespoons tahini
- 2 tablespoons peanut / almond butter
- 1 large apple, cored, thinly sliced
- 1/2 teaspoon ground cinnamon
- 2 tablespoons honey

Method:
1. Apply peanut or almond butter over all the slices of bread.
2. Lay apple slices over it. Put a few drops of honey and tahini at a few places over the apple slices.
3. Sprinkle ground cinnamon and place the prepared sandwiches on a baking sheet.
4. Bake in a preheated oven at 450 degree F for about 5 minutes and serve.

Homemade Burgers

Ingredients:
- 2 eggs
- 2 1/2 pounds ground beef
- 1/2 teaspoon dried minced onion
- 2 tablespoons coconut flour
- 1 teaspoon chili powder
- 1 1/2 teaspoons garlic powder
- 1/4 teaspoon red pepper flakes or to taste
- 1 teaspoon dried oregano
- 1 teaspoon dried basil
- 1/2 teaspoon ground coriander
- Black pepper to taste
- Salt to taste
- Whole wheat burger buns to serve, as required

Method:
1. Mix together all the ingredients with your hands. Shape into patties.
2. Place a nonstick pan over medium heat. Spray with cooking spray. Place patties over it and cook on both the sides.
3. Apply mayonnaise or any spread you desire.
4. Place inside the burger and serve.
5. Place the unused, uncooked burger on a baking sheet and freeze.
6. Once frozen, remove from the baking sheet and place in a freezer safe dish and freeze again.

Chapter 15: Whole foods infused water
Lemon ginger water

Ingredients:
- 1 pitcher water
- 2 large lemons
- 2 inches ginger
- 1 tablespoon honey
- Ice cubes
- Mint leaves

Method:
1. Cut the lemons into thin slices and add to the pitcher of water.
2. Grate the ginger using a fine grater and add to the pitcher.
3. Tear the mint leaves and add to the water.
4. Use a muddler to gently crush all the ingredients so that they release their flavor.
5. Add in honey and stir until well combined.
6. Add in ice cubes and stir until well combined.
7. Serve cold.
8. You can add in some more honey if you desire.

Strawberry basil water

Ingredients:
- 1 cup strawberry, chopped
- 1 cup fresh basil leaves
- 1 pitcher water
- 1 tablespoon honey
- Ice cubes
- Mint leaves

Method:
1. Add the strawberries to the pitcher and stir.
2. Roughly tear the basil leaves and add to the pitcher.
3. Use a muddler to crush the berries and the basil leaves to help them release flavor.
4. Roughly tear the mint leaves and add to the pitcher.
5. Add in honey and mix until everything is well combined.
6. Add in ice cubes and serve cold.

Spicy water

Ingredients:
- 1 inch cinnamon
- 2 cloves
- 2 cardamoms
- ½ inch nutmeg
- 1 large orange
- 1 pitcher water
- 3 tablespoons honey
- Mint leaves
- Ice cubes

Method:
1. Add the cinnamon, cardamom, nutmeg and cloves to a small bowl and use the back of a rolling pin to lightly crush them.
2. Add to the pitcher of water and stir until well combined.
3. Cut the orange into small slices and add to the pitcher of water.
4. Use a muddler to gently crush the spices and orange slices.
5. Stir until the flavor infuses.
6. Roughly tear the mint leaves and add to the pitcher.
7. Add in the honey and mix until well combined.
8. Add ice cubes and mix.
9. Serve cold.

Grapefruit infusion

Ingredients:
- 2 grapefruits
- 1 large lemon
- 1 pitcher water
- 2 tablespoons honey
- Mint leaves
- Ice cubes

Method:
1. Scoop the insides of a grape fruit and add to the pitcher of water.
2. Cut the lemon into thin slices and add to the pitcher.
3. Use a muddler to gently crush all the ingredients.
4. Roughly tear the mint leaves and add to the pitcher.
5. Add in the honey and give everything a good mix.
6. Add in ice cubes and serve cold.

Melon and ginger infusion

Ingredients:
- ½ water melon, chopped
- ½ musk melon, chopped
- ½ inch ginger
- 1 pitcher water
- Mint leaves
- 2 tablespoons honey
- Ice cubes

Method:
1. Add the watermelon to the pitcher and use a muddler to crush it gently.
2. Add in the muskmelon and crush gently.
3. Grate the ginger and add to the pitcher.
4. Tear the mint leaves and add to the pitcher.
5. Mix everything until well combined.
6. Add in honey and give everything a good mix.
7. Add in the ice cubes and stir until well combined.
8. Serve cold.

Banana and Honey infusion

Ingredients:
- 2 large ripe bananas, chopped
- 1 pitcher water
- 2 tablespoons honey
- Mint leaves
- Ice cubes

Method:
1. Chop the bananas and add to the pitcher.
2. Use a muddler to gently crush the fruit. (Be careful not to crush it too much)
3. Add in the honey and give everything a good mix.
4. Add the roughly torn mint leaves along with the ice cubes and give everything a good mix.
5. Serve cold.

Green water

Ingredients:
- ½ cup kale, chopped
- 1 avocado, chopped
- Mint leaves
- 3 tablespoons honey
- 1 pitcher water
- Ice cubes

Method:
1. Roughly chop the kale and add to the pitcher.
2. Use a muddler to gently crush it and mix until it infuses completely.
3. Chop the avocado into small pieces and add to the water.
4. Add in honey and mix until well combined.
5. Tear and add the mint leaves to the pitcher and mix.
6. Add in ice cubes and mix until well combined.
7. Serve cold.

Blueberry and melon infusion

Ingredients:
- 1 cup blueberries, roughly chopped
- ½ melon, chopped
- 2 tablespoons honey
- Mint leaves
- 1 pitcher water
- Ice cubes

Method:
1. Add the blueberries to the pitcher and use a muddler to lightly crush them.
2. Add the melons to the pitcher and do the same.
3. Tear the mint leaves roughly and add to the pitcher.
4. Stir in the honey and add the ice cubes.
5. Serve cold.

Cucumber lemon ginger infusion

Ingredients:
- 1 large cucumber, chopped
- 2 lemons
- ½ inch ginger
- Mint leaves
- 2 tablespoons honey
- Ice cubes

Method:
1. Roughly chop the cucumber and add to the pitcher.
2. Use a muddler to crush it lightly.
3. Add in the sliced lemons and mix everything until well combined.
4. Add the ginger and give everything a good mix.
5. Add in the roughly torn mint leaves along with the honey and mix until everything is well combined.
6. Add the ice cubes and serve cold.

Rose petal infusion

Ingredients:
- 2 cups rose petals, assorted colors
- 2 tablespoons honey
- Mint leaves
- 1 pitcher water
- 1 large lemon

Method:
1. Roughly chop the rose petals and add to the pitcher of water.
2. Use a muddler to gently crush the petals.
3. Add in the honey and mix until well combined.
4. Roughly tear the mint leaves and add to the pitcher.
5. Add in the honey and ice cubes and mix well.
6. Serve cold.

Kiwi and rosemary infusion

Ingredients:
- 2 kiwi fruits, roughly chopped
- 2 sprigs rosemary
- Mint leaves
- 1 pitcher water
- 2 tablespoons honey
- Ice cubes

Method:
1. Add the kiwi to the pitcher and use a muddler to crush it gently.
2. Roughly tear the rosemary and add to the pitcher.
3. Mix everything gently.
4. Tear in the mint leaves and add in the honey.
5. Add the ice cubes and mix until well combined.
6. Serve cold.

Conclusion

I thank you once again for choosing this book and hope you had a good time reading it. The main aim of this book was to educate you on the basics of the Whole foods diet. As you can see, the diet is extremely effective in not just helping you lose weight but can also eliminate the occurrence of illnesses. Your entire body will feel rejuvenated and your mind will remain fresh.

The different recipes mentioned in this book are all simple to make and will help you attain optimum health. But don't limit yourself to just these and experiment with the ingredients to come up with some of your own dishes. We have done our bit by educating you on the topic of whole foods diet and it is now up to you to do the rest.

I wish you luck with your dietary endeavors and hope you attain all your goals.

All the best!

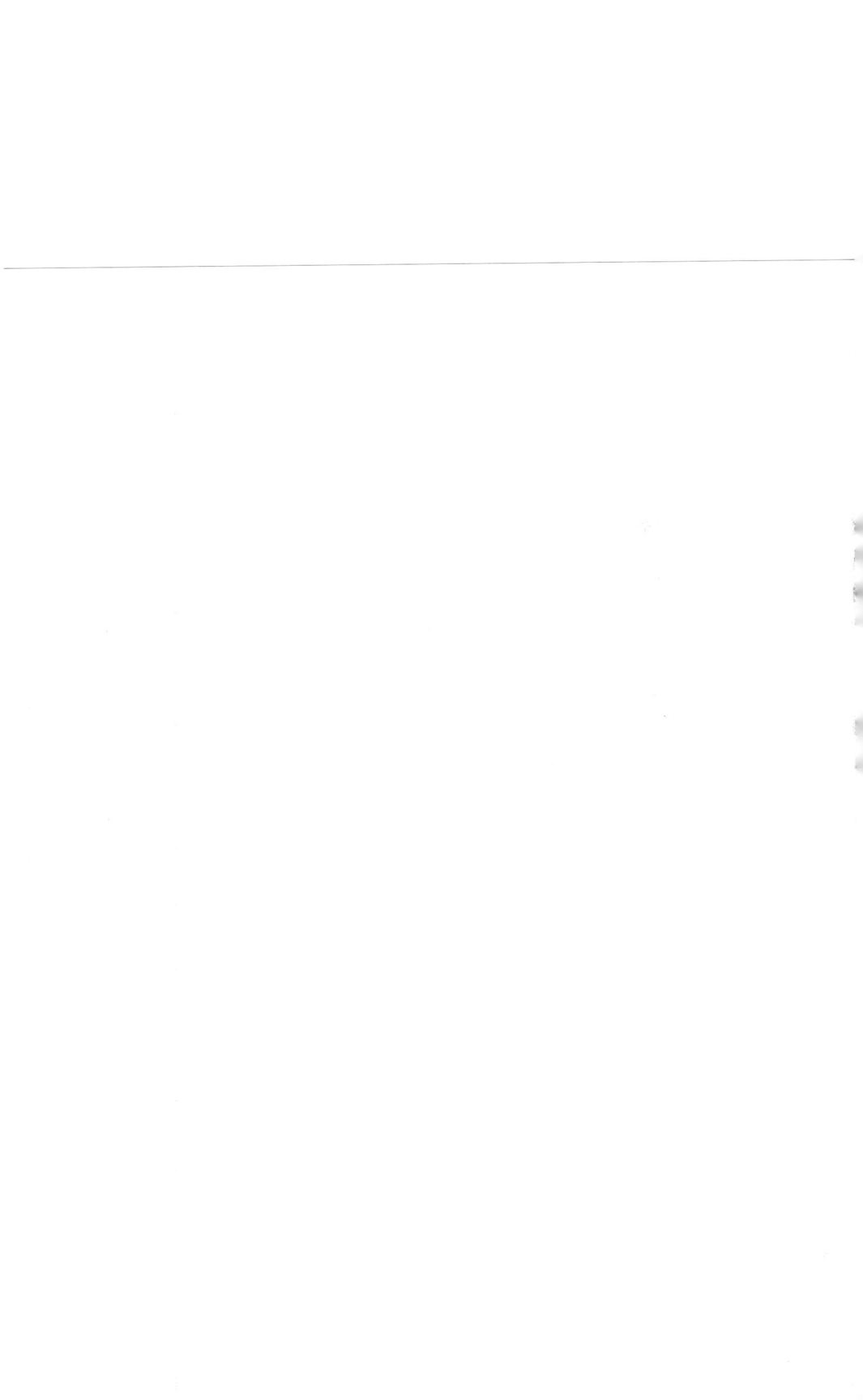

Made in the USA
Lexington, KY
14 November 2016